IN THE
NATIONAL INTEREST

General Sir John Monash once exhorted a graduating class to 'equip yourself for life, not solely for your own benefit but for the benefit of the whole community'. At the university established in his name, we repeat this statement to our own graduating classes, to acknowledge how important it is that common or public good flows from education.

Universities spread and build on the knowledge they acquire through scholarship in many ways, well beyond the transmission of this learning through education. It is a necessary part of a university's role to debate its findings, not only with other researchers and scholars, but also with the broader community in which it resides.

Publishing for the benefit of society is an important part of a university's commitment to free intellectual inquiry. A university provides civil space for such inquiry by its scholars, as well as for investigations by public intellectuals and expert practitioners.

This series, In the National Interest, embodies Monash University's mission to extend knowledge and encourage informed debate about matters of great significance to Australia's future.

Professor Margaret Gardner AC
President and Vice-Chancellor,
Monash University

SAMANTHA CROMPVOETS

BLOOD LUST, TRUST & BLAME

MONASH
UNIVERSITY
PUBLISHING

Blood Lust, Trust & Blame

© Copyright 2021 Samantha Crompvoets

All rights reserved. Apart from any uses permitted by Australia's *Copyright Act 1968*, no part of this book may be reproduced by any process without prior written permission from the copyright owners. Inquiries should be directed to the publisher.

Monash University Publishing
Matheson Library Annexe
40 Exhibition Walk
Monash University
Clayton, Victoria 3800, Australia
https://publishing.monash.edu

Monash University Publishing brings to the world publications which advance the best traditions of humane and enlightened thought.

ISBN: 9781922464613 (paperback)
ISBN: 9781922464620 (ebook)

Series: In the National Interest
Editor: Louise Adler
Project manager & copyeditor: Paul Smitz
Designer: Peter Long
Typesetter: Cannon Typesetting
Proofreader: Gillian Armitage
Printed in Australia by Ligare Book Printers

A catalogue record for this book is available from the National Library of Australia.

The paper this book is printed on is in accordance with the standards of the Forest Stewardship Council®. The FSC® promotes environmentally responsible, socially beneficial and economically viable management of the world's forests.

This book is dedicated to all those who shared their stories with me, and who urged me to look beyond culture.

PREFACE

It is alleged that between 2009 and 2013, Australian Special Forces soldiers unlawfully killed thirty-nine Afghan nationals during incidents that were described to me as competition killing, blood lust, and the glorification of those soldiers who pulled the trigger or directed their subordinates to do so. These were the findings of the *Afghanistan Inquiry Report* released in 2020, based on 'credible evidence'.

The majority of the individuals killed were 'persons under control'. They had either surrendered, been seriously wounded or been captured as prisoners, and they were protected under international laws governing armed conflict and several international conventions to which Australia is a signatory. These alleged murders, committed by Special Forces soldiers—or more accurately, members of the Special Operations Task Groups—are potentially war crimes. They could amount to the worst atrocities ever committed by Australian soldiers.

The details make even the most hardened soldier physically ill, be it from the gruesomeness of the crimes or the shame over how members of their—*our*—armed forces could commit such acts. Repeatedly. Wantonly.

These were deliberate and repeated killings, with the planting of weapons on dead bodies to make it look like the person had been armed. Souvenirs were also taken from deceased Afghan prisoners—a prosthetic leg taken from one was used as a drinking vessel in the barracks for years afterwards. Typically concealable foreign weapons and equipment, such as pistols, small hand-held radios, weapon magazines and grenades, were placed beside the bodies of the 'enemy killed in action' for the purposes of site photography. The intention was to portray the person killed as someone who had been carrying a weapon or other military equipment and therefore was a legitimate target.

Junior Australian soldiers could be required by their patrol commanders to shoot a prisoner, with their first kill known as a 'blooding'. The victims were local nationals—'persons under control'—such as those captured after an attack on a compound, who were legally deemed innocuous and unable to cause harm.

It is alleged that in one account, when a Special Forces patrol landed in an Afghan village in a helicopter, the locals would usually 'squirt'—run away. The soldiers sometimes opened fire, shooting men and sometimes women and children in the back as they ran. The rationale was that these people were making for caches of weapons. The question often asked later was: how many caches did you find? The soldiers always found *something*, or if they didn't, they had a very plausible excuse to explain it. Joint Operations Command, the

Australian Defence Force's operational head-quarters, based in Canberra, heard reports of an ever-increasing number of such 'sanctioned massacres'. The Special Forces soldiers were able to do just enough to have a sufficient basis in law to justify their actions.

Another allegation described how Australian Special Forces personnel would cordon off a whole village, killing those who tried to run away and locking the women and children into houses. Men and boys would be taken to dwellings set aside by the villagers as guesthouses, where they would be interrogated, often tied up and tortured. They might be there for days, and the whole village would be deprived of food, water and medicines. There were no humanitarian corridors available for non-government organisations, no independent observers, no witnesses. After Special Forces had left, men and boys would be found dead, some-times blindfolded, shot in the head or with their throats slit.

In my interviews with soldiers, I was given the clear impression that under these circumstances, they could do anything they wanted to, and they very often did.

What are Australians to make of the revelations that some of our elite soldiers are guilty of war crimes? What can we learn from the ADF's efforts to understand what happened, and to prevent this from happening again?

BLOOD LUST, TRUST & BLAME

There is little doubt that how we behave, how we talk, what we value, and how we lead, all depend on and are drawn from the social, historical and organisational context in which we live. For that reason, definitions of culture—of organisations, of groups—are prolific and rarely definitive. In anthropology and sociology, the way groups think and act, the material objects that shape the way of life of their members, have been examined in organisational settings since the industrial revolution. Prior to that, the genesis of culture studies was wrapped up in colonisation, in examining tribes and what was or wasn't deemed 'civilised'. It was about understanding the 'other'.

With diminished opportunities to study those deemed 'exotic' and 'uncivilised', attention shifted to examine the secret groups—societies, communities and subcultures—that had remained hidden in plain sight: the Freemasons, Neo-Nazis, bikie gangs, Scientology, the Mafia and so on. Tomes are dedicated to understanding their various beliefs, rituals and social structures: their culture.

More recently, 'culture' has been used as a trope to encapsulate all that may be wrong within an organisation. Descriptions of institutional cultures of silence, cover-ups and corruption are pervasive. In the last few years alone, these descriptors have been used to detail problems in Australia's banking sector, its elite sporting clubs, the Church, the military, performing arts and government.

Why do we so often reach for culture to explain organisational issues? Perhaps because it is intuitive to do so. It provides a signpost for organisation-wide characteristics and matters of importance. But does it provide clarity or obscurity when it comes to really understanding a problem? Does it lead to accountability, or is it a barrier to the taking of responsibility? How do you even know when you've achieved cultural change? Should we in fact be considering other ways of analysing and addressing deeply entrenched organisational issues?

In this book you'll find a brief analysis, or rather a critical questioning, of this excessive focus on culture, one that draws on my recent personal experience and role in bringing to light allegations of war crimes committed by Australian Special Forces soldiers in Afghanistan. I'm not going to provide a detailed analysis of rules of engagement or military culture. Rather, it's my belief that the 'culture diagnosis' is problematic in itself. It's too abstract, too unwieldy, and ultimately it blurs accountability and action.

In a decade of ethnographic research on organisational culture, I have learnt that the impact of senior leaders on an organisation's culture is limited. I've realised that, to effect change, you need to understand how power is distributed in an organisation, and you have to dismantle the existing structures. I've come to understand that impactful micro-changes are a surer bet than transformative change programs.

Blood lust, trust and blame were the key themes that emerged in my work on our Special Forces. Blood lust is one characterisation of Special Forces soldiers allegedly perpetrating atrocities in Afghanistan. While it is perhaps not transfer-rable to other Australian organisational contexts, the issues underlying it are: power and control, influence versus authority, bad apples versus the poisoned orchard.

A trust deficit is the end result of institutional misconduct, lack of transparency and botched accountability, and the transformational change programs that attempt to mend these breaches rarely if ever do. This book calls for something more modest, more tangible, and ultimately, more successful.

The question of who to blame, or who to hold to account, often quickly follows the diagnosis of a culture problem. I will consider this in the context of the relationship between individual actions and collective accountability, and I challenge the dominant argument that senior leaders alone set the prevailing organisational culture.

For many institutions, including the ADF, the idea of culture has become both confused and confusing. There is a cultural malaise—a fog of culture. This fog relates to defining culture and changes to it. It has led to a diffusion of accountability when addressing issues of misconduct in organisations, where problems that have been entrenched by history and tradition are inherited but not owned. It has led to an inability to ask the right questions, and uncertainty about what to measure and monitor in order to evaluate potential change. Emerging from this fog are the loudest voices, the 'hot' issues, the individual change 'champions', but does this really lead to sustained improvement?

This fog is not unique to the ADF. It's common in many organisations that seek to overturn outdated yet well-established practices, structures and norms.

WHAT'S THE MATTER
WITH CULTURE?

The first question I ask when approached to do a 'culture review' is for the issue to be described without using the word 'culture'. This word is an easy-to-offer proxy for the hard-to-articulate 'problem', which is usually deeply ingrained, economic or political, or otherwise too hard to see from an internal vantage point.

One of the sources of the word 'culture' is the Latin verb *colere*, meaning to cultivate, nurture, protect. Etymologically it is related to the term 'cult', which is derived from the French *culte*, meaning worship, and which in turn originated from the Latin word *cultus*, meaning care, cultivation, and worship. 'Cult' is probably the most evocative term in this linguistic history—there is a dark side here. What is often not well considered in organisational change efforts is that most forms of collective identity depend on the exclusion of others, sometimes necessarily so. This is where culture starts to become less useful and more complex as a construct for the transformation of organisations.

'Culture' was Merriam-Webster's word of the year in 2014—the word that saw the biggest spike in page views on the publisher's website. One commentator theorised that the jump in those seeking clarification of the word was due to it having become unsettling: 'It used to be a good thing, and now it's not'.[1]

There is no shortage of available words when one needs to describe an organisation's problematic culture. A very quick grab of national news headlines from early 2021 yielded the following:

- banking—risk culture, bad corporate culture, lack of culture, culture of no accountability
- defence—warrior culture, military culture, hypermasculine culture, culture of no transparency
- the Church—culture of secrecy, culture of abuse, culture of concealment
- professional football—competitive culture, culture of racism

- government—culture of corruption, culture
  of bullying, culture of misogyny, toxic
  workplace culture
- performing arts—culture of exploitation,
  culture of discrimination, culture of sexual
  harassment.

Far from its early holistic application, where it was seen as incorporating all knowledge, arts, laws and habits, culture has gone from being something an organisation *is* to something an organisation *has*, 'from being a process embedded in context, to an objectified tool of management control'.[2]

One popular definition of culture is 'the way things are done around here'. This simplification is problematic because it fixes culture problems in the enduring present; it emphasises their stickiness but renders invisible how the issues may have manifested in the first place. It also carries an inflated sense of the ability of leaders to change culture, implying that with the right leader and change management strategy, the way things are done can be altered, and remain so. Yet if culture is so all-encompassing, how can it be changed? Culture is at once everything and therefore nothing.

In 2011, a male cadet at the Australian Defence Force Academy in Canberra filmed himself having sex with a female cadet and broadcast the encounter to others via Skype—all without the female cadet's knowledge. In the wake of the 'Skype scandal', a major Defence review and reform program was undertaken which resulted in the culture change initiative *Pathway to Change*.[3] This was designed, at least in part, as a response to a series of incidents and allegations that had brought the behaviour of ADF personnel into disrepute. It represented a broad-based attempt to improve Defence's culture and hold its leaders accountable for modelling the desired values and behaviours, and for responding appropriately to complaints by personnel. *Pathway to Change* was the first attempt by Defence at a significant culture reform process—what's referred to in management circles as an 'enterprise-level' solution—rather than focusing on a complementary issue, which might be surprising in light of the long history of cultural adjustments at Defence: the inclusion and promotion of females, the treatment of minorities and people with disabilities, and so on. A strong focus of *Pathway to Change* was the treatment of women in the ADF; allegations of abuse, including sexual abuse, and the responses to these; the use of social media and alcohol, especially by ADF personnel; and employment pathways for women as public service employees in Defence.

Yet at the same time as this historic examination of Defence culture was taking place, the worst of the atrocities by Australian Special Forces soldiers were allegedly occurring in Afghanistan. In the *Afghanistan Inquiry Report* prepared in 2020 by the Inspector-General of the Australian Defence Force (IGADF), and in subsequent commentary, 'culture' featured heavily in analyses of what went wrong in Special Forces.[4] With so much attention being paid to understanding culture within the Defence enterprise, how had there been such a significant blind spot? The broader question is: how does any organisation identify its own blind spots?

The fact is that while the concept of culture might be convenient for describing hard-to-pinpoint organisational problems, it is far less useful when it comes to creating genuine change. It becomes an easy way to displace politics and shift blame. Positioning something as a problem of culture can liberate individuals from responsibility. Indeed, I have often heard failures in culture change management described, ironically, as the result of a 'culture of resistance'. It seems there are many places to hide in the all-encompassing realm of culture.

You might be wondering how it is possible to describe issues of child sexual abuse in institutional contexts, sexual assault in the ministerial workplace, or calculated deceit in banking without using the word 'culture'. Admittedly, it can be difficult to avoid this term when describing organisational issues—talking about culture can be intuitive, a useful starting point for signposting problems. However, I argue that you can avoid it—indeed, that you should. Regardless of how authentic and invested senior leadership may be, or how generous the change management budget is, or how lofty the cultural vision statement is, the concept of culture is a flawed framework to use when addressing misconduct.

Furthermore, I believe that refusing to just point a finger at culture ultimately allows for greater clarity and accountability. It lets you scrutinise the specifics of what's going on, and gives you an opportunity to quickly address issues through targeted interventions. On the other hand, the mere blaming of culture only serves to obscure what's happening.

THE PURSUIT OF TRUTH

A go-to catchcry for a particularly vocal group of commentators of late is that the 'fog of war' goes a long way towards explaining, justifying and possibly even excusing the Special Forces atrocities that have come to light. It's a term that seeks to capture the uncertainty regarding one's own capability in battle, the capability of the adversary, and the intent of that adversary during an engagement, operation or campaign. The early nineteenth-century Prussian general Carl von Clausewitz wrote in his book *On War* that war

> is the realm of uncertainty; three quarters of the factors on which action in war is based are wrapped in a fog of greater or lesser uncertainty. A sensitive and discriminating judgment is called for; a skilled intelligence to scent out the truth.[5]

But what kind of truth was Clausewitz talking about?

Among the various kinds of truths, there are two that matter the most here—empirical truth and convenient truth. Empirical truth is based on evidence, research and reason, while convenient truth is based on need, desire and emotion. Can the fog of war be considered a convenient truth in the context of war crimes allegations? Can culture? I argue that the obscure nature of culture lends itself to convenient truths. Empirical truth is harder to establish—it requires rigorous experimentation and critical questioning.

With regard to the Special Forces war crimes allegations, the empirical truth, as I have come to understand it, was less about the heinous misconduct that was occurring for some time, and more about the barriers that prevented it from being seen. The way in which power, and importantly, influence, was distributed in some Special Forces units was at odds with the broader hierarchical command-and-control nature of the organisation. It didn't flow in the way it was expected to—in the way it was taught, trained and, ultimately, taken for granted.

A related truth was that the chain of command had been fractured. The systems and structures, the mechanisms of accountability, were broken. Because this was mostly experienced at the individual level, rather than being objectively observed at the constantly changing organisational level, gaps in knowledge and formal power structures were established. However, this didn't escape unnoticed. It was felt at the external or national level, as evidenced in the interviews I conducted with members of Australia's security community.[6]

I believe that one of the biggest factors in uncovering the issues that were occurring in Special Forces was that I didn't set out to do a culture review. A culture review would have set me on a different path. To begin with, it would have involved speaking to people inside the organisation. I would have been equipped with a line of inquiry based on issues that had already been recognised by senior members of Defence. The behaviour of the interview participants, too, would have been shaped by the mere mention of a culture review. 'Culture' is a trigger word that signals an examination of the 'bad' that is occurring, and participants would have been motivated to emphasise their position in relation to that 'bad'. Those who felt that their experience was not representative of the culture being assessed, who saw their experience as unique, might have been less inclined to share their stories. Many times, I've had interview requests declined for reasons such as 'I'll have nothing to add, I've actually had a good experience so far!'

Rather than being about the Special Operations Command culture, the project for which I was

engaged was about the organisation's capability—
how it functioned.

A SENSE OF DISQUIET

On 14 December 2014, Man Haron Monis held
hostage ten customers and eight employees of the
Lindt Chocolate Café in Martin Place, Sydney,
which led to a sixteen-hour stand-off. When the
sound of a gunshot came from inside the café,
NSW Police officers from the Tactical Operations
Unit stormed the premises. Tori Johnson, the
manager of the café, was killed by Monis, and
one of the customers, Katrina Dawson, was killed
by ricocheting police bullets in the ensuing raid;
Monis was also killed. Three other hostages and
a police officer were wounded by police gunfire
during the raid. As has been widely documented,
the police response to the siege was heavily criti-
cised, and questions were raised about the role that
the Australian Army's 2nd Commando Regiment,
or more specifically the Tactical Assault Group–
East, could or should have played.

The day of the Lindt Chocolate Café siege was also the day that Major General Jeffery Sengelman became the commander of Special Operations Command (SOCOMD). He was now in charge of the Special Forces and its supporting units, reporting variously to the Chief of the Defence Force (domestic counterterrorism), the Chief of Army (with raise, train and sustain functions) and the Chief of Joint Operations (operational functions). Sengelman's first few days in this role were significant in shaping his thinking around the part that SOCOMD played in domestic counterterrorism at that time, and what part it might play in the future. As a result, in mid-2015, I was asked by Sengelman to undertake a review of the external perceptions of SOCOMD. The aim was to provide a snapshot of how well Special Operations integrated, operated and coordinated with other ADF and whole-of-government capabilities in support of Australia's national security. The then Chief of Army, now Chief of the Defence Force, General Angus Campbell, was to extend invitations to participate in the review to senior members of the national security community and to the Defence Senior Leadership Group.

At the time, the request was not a contentious one. I had been doing sociological research on various aspects of Defence since 2009, and for the Chief of Army since 2012. I was practiced at engaging with members of the organisation at all ranks and interviewing high-level external stakeholders. But over the next few months, as I conducted interviews and read into the history of SOCOMD, including the Special Air Service Regiment (SASR) and 2nd Commando Regiment, a palpable silence emerged, and I was left with a sense of disquiet. There was something consistently but very quietly spoken about in the interviews, something alluded to but never detailed. Interview participants didn't refer to issues of culture but rather to sensing 'tensions'.[7] What these perceptions amounted to was a trust deficit that had significant implications for the future of SOCOMD.

It was my disorientation and uncertainty about the meaning of these brief, often quickly dismissed comments that piqued my interest. At this point, I could have diagnosed the problem as one of culture. It fit the parameters of such a problem: ambiguous, perhaps persistent. I decided to speak to insiders in the Special Forces units, but not to understand their views on the units' collective culture—the beliefs, values and perceived norms at work. Rather, I wanted to comprehend how the various parts of Special Forces functioned, and how they had come to be like that. I listened to the individual stories of officers and soldiers, and importantly, I listened to them while they questioned their experiences, their organisation, and their sense of self at that moment.

From this point, as often happens with qualitative inquiry, the list of interview participants snowballed. Word had gone round that I was conducting a review and I began to be contacted directly by both current serving and ex-serving members of SOCOMD, and those who had worked alongside SOCOMD on operations, all of them interested in also being interviewed. Many of these interviews were conducted in the same manner as the earlier ones: face-to-face, confidentially, in an office of some description.

Some people would only agree to be interviewed over the phone, with a few consenting on the proviso that they didn't have to give me their name. In one instance, an anonymous letter was left on my desk in Army headquarters in Canberra. These conversations didn't focus on culture but instead revolved around specific incidents, events, and patterns of behaviour by certain groups of people. Many of those I spoke with were deeply affected because of the incongruence of the alleged heinous behaviour compared with their own personal and professional sense of identity and integrity—it was because they knew these behaviours didn't fit with the organisation they belonged to that they felt compelled to share their stories with me.

The attitudes of individual soldiers and the atrocities they may or may not have committed were one thing. Why these things hadn't been uncovered or examined before was quite another. I reported the former and sought to understand the latter.

The IGADF's inquiry into questions of unlawful conduct concerning Australian Special Forces soldiers in Afghanistan concluded that there were thirty-six matters to be referred to the Australian Federal Police; that there had been twenty-three incidents which encompassed thirty-nine unlawful killings; and that nineteen individuals had been involved. The author of the *Afghanistan Inquiry Report*, Major General the Honourable Paul Brereton, gives culture as a key explanatory factor, describing a 'cultural disconnect'. He talks about a 'warrior culture', 'warrior hero culture', 'warrior hero culture of killing', a 'culture of secrecy', a 'culture of silence', a 'culture of compartmentalisation', 'tribal culture', a 'cultured normalisation of deviance', the 'need to encourage a culture of honesty', a 'culture of non-reporting', dependencies on 'force element culture', a 'culture of command non-inquiry', 'special forces culture' and a 'culture of cover-ups'. He also points to 'failures of culture' and a 'culture that has departed from acceptable norms', and refers to the 'prevailing organisational culture' (not defined). There is also mention of a 'culture of command-supported interference and resistance toward ADF investigators', a 'culture which promotes, permits or prohibits certain behaviours', a 'culture of deference to patrol commanders', and a 'Special Operations Task Group culture that permitted the behaviours described in the report'.

In the report, culture is specifically described as 'bred', 'embraced', 'propagated', 'shaped' and 'fostered'. In this sense, it is positioned as something that can be manoeuvred, something that is malleable, changeable. But it is also situated as an independently existing phenomenon—it promotes, permits or prohibits certain behaviours.

While the report makes many valid and important observations, it also raises many questions. Who or what, for instance, does the embracing and propagating? Does culture shape or is it being shaped, or both? When does it stop being shaped and when does it start shaping? Where do you aim an intervention? It seems clear that while culture might be a handy trope, its ambiguity prevents the right questions from being asked about the symptomatic misconduct. In turn, it is defined by these symptoms; for example, sexual harassment in the performing arts is a 'culture of sexual harassment'; child sexual abuse in the Church is 'a culture of abuse'. In shifting the problem to the macro level, it is presented as a generalised phenomenon, and it then becomes a 'thing' to blame. Individual accountability is obscured.

The pursuit of truth is a lofty way to describe my approach to the SOCOMD review. I could just say that I was seeking to answer the question that was weighing heavily on me: what the fuck is going on? It has been said that there is no such thing as truth. There is merely a diversity of narratives and interpretations. I believe this to be accurate, and it explains to me why the construct of culture is so comforting: it is a handy catch-all concept.

The soldiers whom I interviewed often described their peers as having 'blood lust', which was about violence, power and control. Much beyond this remains unclear. Perhaps the reasons why certain individuals committed the alleged atrocities can be discovered by deeply examining the interconnections between 'just war theory' (an attempt to figure out when it's OK to go to war), failures in military ethics, psychopathic tendencies, toxic masculinity, the normalisation of deviance and so on. Certainly this is beyond the scope of this book, but undoubtedly it will be the subject of many to come.

Understanding how incidents of misconduct relate to the culture of the Defence organisation is even more complicated. The culture did not make those involved commit the atrocities. If that had been the case, then many more of the thousands of soldiers who deployed would surely also have committed them. So was there a culture problem? It could be argued that something isn't 'cultural' unless it is a whole-of-organisation phenomenon. A culture of misconduct can explain the average tendency of participants to commit misconduct, but it cannot explain any variance in participation.

The sociologist Stjepan Meštrović extended the 'a few bad apples' metaphor in his analysis of the trials of Abu Ghraib, the prison complex just outside Baghdad that was utilised by the United States after the Iraqi invasion. He described sources of contamination in the 'poisoned orchard' and the culpability of the 'orchard keepers'—the civilians and officers high in the chain of command. Instead of culture, he referred to abusive climates, abusive atmospheres and abusive relationships. While it is tempting to cut and paste one analysis of peer military crimes of war atop another, Meštrović's detailed study does not easily lend itself to comparisons with the context of Australian Special Forces misconduct. His examination of Abu Ghraib described 'egregious social disorganization and chronic, persistent social chaos', which, he argued, inevitably led to abuse.[8] The soldiers involved in Abu Ghraib were not from an elite soldiering cadre, had relatively little social capital, and were reportedly living in squalor comparable to that of the prisoners. In contrast, the Australian Special Forces soldiers were better trained, better resourced, better fed and better equipped by a considerable factor greater than the Australian Regular Army, and certainly those they detained.

Special Forces, unlike their Regular Army counterparts, are strategic both as a national instrument of martial force and as a high-value asset in the battle-space. Their capabilities are very often cloaked in extreme secrecy, not even known to the majority of the ADF. They have variously been described as phantoms of the jungle, elite operators, and, importantly, as strategically and tactically invisible during combat operations. Accordingly, a comparison with the questionably mitigating circumstances of Abu Ghraib, or excusing them through an explanation of the fog of war, is reductive and militarily naive. To the contrary, it could be argued that there is a greater expectation that during the fog of war these soldiers would rise to the challenge of scenting out the truth and undertaking complex military actions with extreme stealth and precision.

What is analogous to Abu Ghraib, however, is that the details of the alleged atrocities in Afghanistan have now become background noise, as they were in the US trials, media and overall discourse. Already, Australian commentary on the Special Forces war crimes has shifted from details of the alleged wrongdoing, including murder, to concerns about the loss of medals, the legacies of SASR veterans from World War II, and a personal, professional and symbolic betrayal of Australia's veterans, diggers and elite 'dogs of war' by Defence's top brass.

THE DISTRIBUTION OF POWER

There are a number of alternatives to culture theories when it comes to understanding misconduct in or by organisations. In respect of Australia's Special Forces, a focus on power is likely to have the most impact. Understanding how power operates within an organisation enables you to move beyond observing the problems. It allows you to focus resources—time, effort, money and goodwill—where they can have the greatest effect. In other words, instead of trying to orchestrate a whole-of-organisation transformation, which so often is doomed to fail, moving beyond culture enables targeted interventions.

The distribution of power within and across Defence has rarely been discussed when it comes to the organisation's culture. Military power is most often talked about in terms of effectiveness and capability. In contrast, so-called soft power refers to persuasion through public diplomacy, economic or political influence. Looking at power rather than culture yields very different insights and different choices in the action you can subsequently take.

Defence is an organisational and bureaucratic behemoth, comprising not just the three services of Navy, Army and Air Force, but also twelve separate groups across the Defence Public Service, including the Defence People Group, Defence Science and Technology Group, Estate and Infrastructure Group, Capability Acquisition and Sustainment Group, Joint Capabilities Group and Defence Intelligence Group. The Australian Army comprises four functional commands, all reporting to the Chief of Army—SOCOMD is one of these four, alongside the 1st Division, Forces Command and the Australian Army Cadets. SOCOMD is made up of the SASR, based in Perth; the 1st Commando Regiment (made up of mostly Army

Reserves) based in Sydney and Melbourne; and the 2nd Commando Regiment, the Special Operations Engineer Regiment and the Special Operations Logistics Squadron, also Sydney-based. In addition, there is the Special Operations Training and Education Centre, also located in Sydney, as well as the Parachute Training Centre in Nowra, New South Wales.

The media reporting on war crimes allegations has usually referred to 'Special Forces' more broadly, which technically refers to any or all of the units that make up SOCOMD. More specifically, recent allegations pointedly relate to Force Elements drawn from the SASR when deployed as part of a Special Operations Task Group (SOTG). A complete explanation of the Australian Special Operations structure and workings is outside the scope of this book, but I can provide some definitional colour here to make the context clearer.

From the top, there is a convoluted, but necessary authority relationship that needs to be understood. The first tenet is that the Chief of Army, contrary to popular belief, does not command the operations of the Australian Army, including SOCOMD. He is responsible for the raising, training and sustaining of the Army. For any employment of the military, first, the National Security Committee of government must agree to the need, scope and parameters of the intervention. The Chief of the Defence Force, who ultimately commands all ADF military forces, exercises his command and control authorities via the Commander of Joint Operations Command, a three-star lieutenant-general (or equivalent) officer who is in the ADF's military command and control centre, which is located in a former sheep paddock near Bungendore, New South Wales that has been fitted out with very high razor-wire fences and cameras.

A SOTG is a specifically structured bespoke organisation that draws from all of the ADF's assets as deemed necessary, to build a potent, fit-for-purpose special operations combat unit. It is a transient task-oriented organisation, or more accurately a temporary set of 'capability bricks'.

The majority of personnel are usually drawn from within SOCOMD. The size and composition of these SOTGs can vary. However, it is usual that they are commanded by an O5-ranked officer (rank of lieutenant-colonel), and more often than not a Special Operations lieutenant-colonel. It's noteworthy that SOCOMD has a number of standing SOTGs that are pre-constituted, trained, exercised and ready to execute specific contingency plans such as counterterrorism, shock action and special recovery operations.

Special Operations Force Elements can vary in size and capability. A 'patrol' is the smallest of the capability bricks that make up a SOTG. These are usually 4–5-person teams commanded by a sergeant (sometimes a senior corporal). They are highly trained, highly lethal and usually highly disciplined, and can operate clandestinely and in a decentralised way. Three patrols are commanded by a troop, which itself is nominally commanded by an O3-ranked officer. In practice, however, the actual command authority and agency of this relatively junior captain is challenged by the fact that it is the sergeants who exercise real command, mostly due to their experience, loyalty from other soldiers, and the fellowship and time spent with others from this small unit. Contrast this to the captain troop commander, who has authority by virtue of his/her rank and appointment, but no agency due to their relative lack of experience when compared with the sergeants.

This difference between actual and nominal command authority proved significant in the events that gave rise to the Afghanistan inquiry, making clear the relevance of understanding actual power distribution, with important consequences for accountability.

ASKING THE RIGHT QUESTIONS

A common mistake when using culture as an anchor for change programs is that it often results in a focus on one or a selection the many descriptors of the 'bad' culture, and they are likely to be symptoms rather than root causes. A toxic workplace culture might be related to the lack of a robust complaints management process; a culture of bullying could be due to structures that assimilate rather than integrate; a culture of corruption might have more to do with weak regulatory systems.

My approach to asking questions to understand how a problem manifested in the first place is similar to the adage about tying knots. If you don't know how to tie one, tie many. Sociology is useful here because it asks questions from multiple vantage points. There are a number of layers and perspectives that come in handy when trying to understand an organisation. One is the lived experience—an individual's expectations, perceptions, their day-to-day reality.

Then there's the organisational perspective. In the Defence context, this can be at the service level, such as the Army, Airforce, Navy or public service. Or it could be a smaller cluster such as SOCOMD. This is a collective vantage point. It is defined by an agreed set of values, norms and rituals. There are similarities in the pathways to promotion: what is rewarded, what is valued. When people join, they join Army, Navy or Airforce, or the Australian Public Service—not 'Defence'—and their organisational identity is shaped accordingly.

And finally there's the external or national/political layer. This includes high-level perspectives, such as that of government, or of the public as it is represented by the media or elsewhere. It's about a broader vantage point that takes in more than just what's occurring at the organisational level.

All of these levels interact. The legislation passed by government is implemented differently in policies at the organisational level and can be experienced quite differently by individuals. Things can also be shaped from the bottom up. One person's experience, and how the organisation responds to it, can have enduring implications at an external or political level. One example is the February 2021 allegation that, in March 2019, a former Liberal staffer for Defence Minister Linda Reynolds was raped in the minister's office in Parliament House by a male colleague. Another is the ADFA Skype scandal. Yet another is a cricket player's use of sandpaper to gain a competitive advantage.

In trying to understand organisational problems—pursuing the truth—there are constant tensions between empirical and convenient truth, between evidence and emotion. But there are also tensions between time and resources, political will and individual needs. As tempting as it is to summarise organisational problems in terms of the resultant 'culture', I am interested in a different question: how does power operate, both formally and informally, within and between all the different levels? Ask 'who' has power and also ask 'what' has power. How does that power shape, influence and obstruct? In the case of Special Forces, how accountability is viewed and experienced differs between, for example, a patrol commander, a SOTG or Special Operations commander, and the National Security Committee.

It is only when you examine issues in this way that you can begin to unravel why certain problems persist, or why they go unnoticed. What emerges are the influential sources of power and knowledge and what in fact sustains them. It is often assumed in institutions, particularly large and historically male-dominated ones, that power is distributed hierarchically, but the situation is more complex and contested than that.

Trying to discover the root cause of an issue and how it manifested in the first place is the key to understanding and being able to address an organisational problem. Comprehending how different symptoms of a culture might be related requires a process of critical questioning, not just of the organisation but of its context. You need to examine the relationship between power and accountability, and look closely at social networks and organisational climate rather than culture. This provides an alternative framework for understanding how and where misconduct occurs in an organisation, and importantly, how it spreads.

THE POLITICS OF ACCOUNTABILITY

Since the release of the IGADF's *Afghanistan Inquiry Report*, accountability has been a topic debated with high emotion. The details of the alleged war crimes were quickly usurped by public and political commentary on this subject, with the discourse rapidly shifting to who to blame. In the report, Paul Brereton refers to a 'hierarchy of relative criminal responsibility'. Is accountability hierarchical as well? Or is it more complicated than that when accountability mechanisms have been actively undermined?

The concept of organisational culture is problematic when it comes to questions of accountability. Social networks and organisational climate are actually more practical frameworks for diagnosing issues and targeting change efforts. It pays to focus on the local rather than the overarching, on influence rather than authority. When something goes wrong at the overarching level of institutional culture, for example, who is to blame? When that problem breaches the trust of the Australian community, how can it be rebuilt?

The question of accountability looms large when misconduct occurs in an organisation, particularly if it relates to a culture of misconduct.

This question differs from 'Who is responsible?' Accountability as a construct is almost as ambiguous as culture when it comes to trying to define causal relationships or to address deficits, often leading to calls for greater transparency or for a senior leader or leaders to fall on their sword. Questions of accountability mechanisms, systems, regimes and frameworks, debates about individual versus collective accountability, distinctions between accountability and responsibility, answerability and liability, the relationship of accountability to governance or regulation—all of these create confusion, not clarity.

Research commissioned by the Royal Commission into Institutional Responses to Child Sexual Abuse found that cultures can be built from the bottom up (from lower-level employees) or from the top down (from upper-level officials).[9] They can even develop from side to side, emanating from the constituencies the organisation serves and those that give it external support. This could be said of the veteran and ex-service organisation community that sits outside of any formal Defence structures yet remains highly influential. Similarly, it could be said of ex-service members who join defence industry or management consulting firms only to consult back to Defence on issues of culture and change management.

A literature review of five decades of empirical research on accountability found that we are yet to achieve a clear understanding of the causal effects of accountability on individual decision-making and behaviour, and the outcomes of those activities.[10] Similar to culture, it is easier to point to failures in accountability rather than to instances where accountability mechanisms have led to the desired outcomes. Can being accountable be defined as being answerable for the actions taken within one's sphere of influence, or is it something more?

Detailed research into the definitions of both accountability and responsibility has concluded that the confusion between these concepts is a failure to separate the obligation to satisfactorily perform a task (responsibility) from the liability to ensure that it is satisfactorily done (accountability).[11] In the case of Special Forces, it could be that the soldiers on the ground had responsibility, whereas the higher chain of command had accountability, as they provide the scaffolding that sets everything up for success or failure. However, this framing does not take into account authority relative to influence. As was established in the findings of the Afghanistan Inquiry, and described in my related reports, in the context of Special Forces, power was concentrated at the lower rank of patrol commander.

Many real-world examples of misconduct involve multiple individuals linked by social ties, or networks. For example, in the banking sector, the networks can include regulators, bank executives, lenders, borrowers, boards and the ombudsman. In sporting clubs, they can include the players, player associations, managers, club administrators, fans, betting agencies and code administrators. The ties between them can be formal and informal, visible and invisible. They can be facilitated and reinforced through shared histories, geographical location or socialisation.

But while influence can occur within a social network, the individuals in it don't necessarily need to be co-located. This was evident in the analyses of what occurred at Abu Ghraib that also pointed to a widespread pattern of abuse, indeed a climate of abuse, at the Guantánamo Bay detention facility in Cuba, in Afghanistan, and elsewhere in Iraq. Meštrović argues that it takes some 'magical thinking' to believe that corrupt soldiers in these locations spontaneously invented remarkably similar methods of committing abuse.[12] When misconduct spreads throughout an organisation, it can be said to characterise the organisation as a whole—sometimes, misconduct can spread between organisations via social networks.

A cultural analysis asks questions related to beliefs, attitudes and values, whereas a network analysis examines how things like knowledge and influence operate in an organisation. Rather than looking at what incidences of misconduct occur, you examine how they spread.

Academic research has demonstrated that deviations from broader norms of conduct are likely to be particularly strong in the parts of a network that are densely connected internally but relatively isolated from the rest of the network. These isolated cliques are especially capable of developing distinct norms and behaviours. Henrich Greve summarises this as follows: internally well-connected and globally isolated parts of a network are likely to engage in misconduct.[13] This description fits SASR patrols: small groups of four to five soldiers who are part of a small Special Forces deployment, and who are physically separated from the Regular Army while on base. This is replicated at a different scale in the physical dislocation of Special Forces units in Perth when the majority of the Army units are situated on Australia's north and east coasts.

Power and knowledge, or rather the concealment of knowledge—secrecy—are two significant predictors of misconduct that can be seen in a number of institutional contexts. In the case of the Catholic Church, for example, the sanctity of the confessional combined with cloistered isolation and a centralised power structure allowed miscreant clergy to exploit failings in transparency. Special Forces units might be at one extreme in terms of secrecy, but many organisations have dark, albeit less-elite corners.

When poor or undesirable behaviours are institutionalised, they are embedded in organisational memory, solidified in routines and structures. A culture of misconduct then develops. In particular, misconduct will be facilitated by the selection of employees who are receptive to engaging in wrongdoing or who are susceptible to social influences. In the case of elite units like Special Forces, and similar units in police forces, the high value and tight control of the selection course is potentially problematic.

The more elite, secretive and cloistered a group is, the higher the chance of deviation, and the concealment of that deviation. This is exacerbated when that group or subgroups hold specialist skills that are not well understood by those outside the organisation, and are revered or despised. If culture reform initiatives do not dismantle or defuse these aspects of power and control, influence and secrecy, then organisational change will not occur—and if it does, it won't be sustained.

CLIMATE, NOT CULTURE

The concept of climate is far more practical to apply than culture when it comes to organisational misconduct—or, in fact, when trying to understand any organisational issue. It takes into account the fact that behaviours or attitudes at the lower levels of an organisation may not manifest at a higher level. Unlike culture, the organisational climate can quite literally change overnight, usually with a change in leadership. The leader can set the climate in their local environment, which is often reflected in descriptions of morale, engagement and productivity.

Organisational climate is not explicitly mentioned in the *Afghanistan Inquiry Report* (redacted parts notwithstanding). However, the report does describe a palpable frustration that refers to the climate of the Special Operations Task Group:

[I]t has been written that commanders set the conditions in which their units may flourish or wither, including the culture which promotes, permits or prohibits certain behaviours. It is clear that there must have been within SOTG a culture that at least permitted the behaviours described in the report. However, that culture was not created or enabled in SOTG, let alone by any individual SOTG Commanding Officer. Because SOTG was a task group drawn from multiple troop contributing units and multiple rotations, each SOTG Commanding Officer acquired a mix of personnel with which he had little prior influence or exposure. There was little opportunity for the Commanding Officer of any SOTG rotation to create a SOTG culture.[14]

Indeed, the SOTG commander couldn't set the culture. But they could challenge and influence the climate. Arguably, however, this was done by the patrol commanders, who had significant influence over subordinates as well as over SOTG commanders. There was a formal command authority downward and an informal, yet significant influence upward (and arguably sideways). Patrol commanders controlled the flow of knowledge and in doing so were incredibly empowered to set the parameters of what was normal in terms of processes and procedures. As verified in the *Afghanistan Inquiry Report*, 'upstream, higher headquarters received a misleading impression of operations, and downstream, operators and patrol commanders knew how to describe an incident in order to satisfy the perceived reporting requirements'.[15] In other words, managing up by massaging the message was routine.

In his response to the IGADF inquiry, Angus Campbell spoke of the need for individual *and* collective accountability. The latter referred to all those who had served on operations as part of a SOTG and who were subsequently awarded a Meritorious Unit Citation. This citation, worn on a uniform like a medal, is awarded to recognise a unit as a whole when it achieves 'sustained outstanding service in warlike operations'. Because the accountability mechanisms within Defence lend themselves to individual and hierarchical controls, holding to account all of those who deployed with an SOTG over a period of many years is a very visible and symbolic gesture. But it has received an intense backlash as Afghanistan veterans argue for their own individual freedom from blame.

Again, the focus here on an overarching culture has not helped. Experiences or knowledge of war crimes and other atrocities were not a part of the culture that most soldiers belonged to. However, they were a part of the social network, and it was within this network that misconduct spread— for example, drinking from a deceased Afghan prisoner's prosthetic leg, and other notable customs. Social networks can operate regardless of the functional structure of an organisation, which also means that a restructure won't necessarily work if it doesn't challenge problematic social networks, formal or informal.

Demonstrating improvements in accountability, and therefore transparency, can assist an organisation to regain trust from community or consumer groups. But this isn't very effective if the improvements aren't focused at the level where that breach of trust has occurred. Strengthened corporate governance in banking is great, but does that necessarily increase my trust at the local, individual level? If anything, the trickle-down effect of strengthened banking regulations is experienced at the personal level as delays in getting approved for a loan and incredibly burdensome administrative requirements.

Also, if you're going to measure accountability, then it's important to define it, or to agree on a definition. Otherwise, if a lack of accountability is highlighted as a cultural problem, how do you know when you've fixed it? And when accountability is being measured alongside culture, as it so often is, these definitions become even more important.

From 2011 onwards, a number of independent but related reviews took place that highlighted how the Department of Defence has grappled with concepts of accountability, especially in relation to leadership behaviours. The January

2011 Review of Accountability and Governance in the Defence Department—known as the Black Review because it was led by associate professor Rufus Black—found that accountability system failures had led to poor outcomes, including a failure to deliver capability projects, inappropriate procurement decision-making, and a lack of general cost-consciousness in management. The review pointed out that changes to these mechanisms, while necessary, were insufficient: 'To make changes in accountability "stick", Defence needs to address underlying culture and skills issues ...'[16]

The year of the Black Review also saw the release of *Pathway to Change*, and then, in 2014, the First Principles Review, which was focused on organisational effectiveness and efficiency but positioned as highly dependent on culture and accountability. These documents provide useful demonstrations of how Defence's busyness around culture and accountability potentially obscured both in relation to leadership.

There were three distinct ways in which leadership and accountability were routinely discussed in Defence publications that set out the aims and objectives of the department's culture change journey. There were debates around leadership accountability as a lever for changes to diversity and inclusion; for example, in *Pathway to Change*. Leadership accountability was also spoken of as an expectation that Defence leaders would demonstrate a broad set of appropriate behaviours. And finally, leadership accountability was assessed as a set of expectations that leaders would not only comply with but also model best-practice corporate and governance decision-making, as set out in the Black Review and the First Principles Review—in other words, make decisions in the right ways, leading to improved corporate outcomes.

There are many examples in Defence organisational documents, reviews and annual reports where leadership accountability is discussed in terms of behaviours. Indeed, the focus on behaviours is the most explicit definition of leadership accountability in Defence texts. *Pathway to Change* offers one such example of this:

The Pathway to Change speaks to all in the organisation and asks each individual to hold him or herself to account for their actions. However, it has a particular message for anyone in any type of leadership position: you have a particular responsibility to model agreed values and behaviours, to do your utmost to ensure that those in your charge do likewise, and to take seriously any signs that there are problems that need to be addressed. Leaders will be held especially accountable for how they exercise their authority in this respect.[17]

If an understanding of leadership accountability as a set of behaviours is adopted, then an evaluation would focus on whether leaders are being held to account for their behaviours and for the behaviours that they expect and accept of members among the staff that they manage. If, however, leadership accountability is understood as improved corporate and governance decision-making, then the evaluation would focus on whether the decision-making structures are becoming more streamlined and whether decision-makers are being held to account for the outcomes of their corporate and governance choices.

How accountability is defined determines how it is measured. These nuances, while they might seem semantic, have significant implications when you're trying to achieve change, transparency and ultimately cultural reform. A detailed assessment of how, where and why accountability measures were faulty, and where and whose trust has been breached in the process, will inform how improvements to accountability can be measured and communicated. Without this, a considerable amount of time and money is likely to be wasted trying to understand things that ultimately aren't relevant to the questions that are being asked. In addition, blind spots will remain.

Breaches of trust and public and political debates about blame are highly correlated with diagnoses of culture problems. How power operates within networks can often be at odds with how accountability is structured within an organisation. This can become a widespread source of conflict.

Looking at climate and networks rather than culture creates a significant opportunity to better understand risks and how conducive an environment might be to misconduct. If the misconduct is not a generalised organisational phenomenon, then whole-of-organisation broad-brush culture transformation is likely to be very costly and ineffective, and it will prompt a backlash from those who don't relate to that culture.

THE CONSEQUENCES OF ACTION

Regardless of how much time, money and effort is spent on culture change programs, unless the underlying structures that determine people's behaviours are altered, then any attitudinal or other changes are at best temporary. In addition to this, culture change efforts get distracted by peripheral issues that, even though they aren't central to the underlying problem, are the focus of an intensely felt sense of identity and belonging. Labelling something as a culture issue is a red flag. It is emotive—people are protective of *their* culture, and that includes how it is defined.

At the time of writing, the recommendations to address the findings of the IGADF inquiry had only just been considered and were in the early stages of being actioned. Yet already there is resistance. This is not emanating from those who allegedly committed the crimes but rather from those associated with the units involved and the veterans who served in Afghanistan more broadly and their supporters.

Backlash and disquiet have been key aspects of another reform program in Defence—increasing gender diversity. This example is useful as it illustrates how a cultural problem has been defined and addressed, and demonstrates the unforeseen consequences of those actions.

I have often wondered how the recommendations and insights in the Australian Human Rights Commission's Defence review might have differed if, instead of focusing on women, the commission had examined the treatment of power in the Australian Defence Force Academy and the ADF more broadly.[18] How could an examination of power assist in understanding institutional misconduct? It could be argued that any examination of gender necessarily involves the analysis of power. The report has played a valuable role in increasing awareness about the situation of women in Defence. However, I think an opportunity was missed to be more explicit about the power dynamics beyond gender.

There were many reforms made as a result of the AHRC review; for example, a considerably strengthened complaints management process, and the implementation of the Sexual Misconduct and Prevention Office. Overall, the focus of change was on increasing the participation and promotion of women; removing barriers to recruitment and retention, including gender restrictions for combat roles; and achieving that elusive critical mass. But despite a decade of dedicated undertakings to increase women's participation, progress has been very, very slow.

With so much genuine effort, millions of dollars spent on introspection and change programs, and authentic leaders at the helm, should or could we have expected more change? Should there be greater numbers of women in the workforce? Or is it just that women really don't want to be in the military? Could the outcome have been different if the focus was on women's empowerment as opposed to women's participation? What if the backlash over gender politics wasn't framed as resistance to culture change but as a felt—experienced and perceived—redistribution of power, and for some (men), a sense of loss and letting go? Could there have been more empathy for this, and could communication strategies have been designed accordingly? This discussion is of course an entire book in itself.

Audre Lorde's profound words come to mind: 'The master's tools will never dismantle the master's house'. It might seem out of place, in a book about culture and war crimes, to quote a renowned black lesbian feminist poet delivering a scathing critique of white academic feminism, but I beg to differ.

To bring her quote into context,

> survival is not an academic skill. It is learning how to stand alone, unpopular and sometimes reviled, and how to make common cause with those others identified as outside the structures in order to define and seek a world in which we can all flourish. It is learning how to take our differences and make them strengths. For the master's tools will never dismantle the master's house. They may allow us temporarily to beat him at his own game, but they will never enable us to bring about genuine change. And this fact is only threatening to those women who still define the master's house as their only source of support.[19]

Lorde is reminding us of the importance of structures, of difference, and their relationship to change. That is, you cannot simply create change by using the same mechanisms, processes and tools that have been used to oppress—that have created the issue in the first place. In the case of Special Forces, any changes or actions that reinforce those 'internally well-connected and globally isolated' structures will likely fail, be they geographical, philosophical or administrative.

Organisational structures are the scaffolding that holds culture firmly in place. I'm not referring to hierarchical, organisational or functional charts that illustrate roles and ranks, but rather the legislation, policies, standard operating procedures, remuneration models, performance management frameworks, and sometimes even the physical locations of buildings and/or parts of an organisation. Even after leaders have moved on and change programs have run their course, this scaffolding still supports the underlying power structure. Military coups can be enacted again and again because in countries with governments that are prone to being overthrown, it's very difficult to dismantle the scaffolding that holds the military in a place of power: think Fiji, Myanmar, the Philippines and Pakistan, just to name a few.

To change culture, you need to change the rules of the game and the nature of the field it's played on. These are the stated and unstated rules that determine who gets what, who does what, and who decides—change them and you change how power is distributed. Empowerment means a transformation in power relations. Specifically, it means control over resources: physical, human, intellectual and intangible. It means control over ideology: beliefs, values and attitudes. And it means changes in the institutions and structures that support the inequality of power.

One of the most significant and impactful changes made in the ADF in recent times was not the implementation of recommendations from multiple reviews of the treatment of women and observations of culture, but the change in legislation that enabled part-time service. Under a little-known reform program called Plan Suakin, a small cadre of Defence intellectuals, coincidentally also led by Paul Brereton, undertook some of the most noteworthy dismantling of structural scaffolding in the history of Defence, a framework that had been in place for over 100 years. Prior to this change, no member of the ADF could legally work part-time. They could be employed in the Defence Reserves or they could be employed in the full-time force, but if they wanted to reduce their hours or days they had to apply for something called 'part-time leave without pay'. This was because the *Defence Act* of 1903 stated that all members of the Regular Army and Permanent Navy and Air Force were 'bound to render' continuous full-time service. This most obviously affected women who might want to work less than full-time when combining work and family commitments. Because of the stigma around being less than 'full-time committed', and the historical treatment of reservists as second-class citizens because of this, there was a less than 2 per cent uptake of the leave without pay policy.

Previously, going back as far as the 1950s, there had been many reviews and debates on achieving a 'total force' construct; that is, an ADF that used, and arguably respected, both the Regular/Permanent forces and the Reserve forces as a whole capability, rather than a relatively fragmented one. The proposed altering of the 'bound to render' construct in the *Defence Act 1903*, which was tabled in the federal parliament in early 2015, represented the most significant attempt at a total force in the ADF's history. This wasn't about reducing the liability to serve but rather establishing the flexibility to serve in different and valued ways. Defence's war-fighting capability was retained—contrary to the predictions of many detractors—and indeed strengthened by increasing the ability to call upon different components of the total workforce. If those who were part-time are obligated to serve when needed, then the jibes and warnings regarding a part-time commitment could, and should, erode.

Arguably, the reason this particular change was successful was that Brereton and his judicial colleague, the Victorian judge and fellow Army Reserve Major General Greg Garde QC, cleverly decided not to dismantle the house by using the tools of the master, which could be described as the mantra of unrestricted capability for wartime.

Instead, they used their own tools of law and justice to achieve it.

When it comes to gender diversity in the military, the countries that perform better and are improving, in terms of recruitment and retention, are overwhelmingly those that have embraced policies to remove structural barriers to participation by all segments of the workforce, and that have equitably valued and remunerated those segments. Vison statements are not enduring, nor are statements of values. In fact, frameworks of any kind don't generally last—if they haven't been widely internalised, they might leave the building as soon as the leader who endorsed them leaves. Structures shape behaviours, directly and indirectly, which means that deep structural change in turn develops a capability for more change. Defence has done this when it comes to gender, although its efforts need to be supported by evidenced-based and targeted interventions focused on empowerment rather than participation, along with evaluations of their effectiveness, lest it ends up on a pathway to the status quo.

A final point on the taking of action is that while culture is all-encompassing, it is also made up of small, everyday habits and choices. Large-scale culture transformation can be the first-choice response to addressing organisational problems, but while it can take years to achieve, there is often a rush to see results as quickly as possible. The enduring power structures then undermine the effort by minimising the capability of the organisation to change. The focus is on leaders championing the new plan, while ignoring key influencers in the organisation who may be relatively junior. Also, culture change initiatives are often too conceptual and don't translate easily into everyday actions and tasks. If underlying power dynamics are creating organisational issues, then structural change can shape and reinforce behaviours in a way that will address the problems. Although the change may not miraculously manifest, it can prevent the organisation from defaulting back to problematic norms and practices.

In order to make the kinds of small changes I'm talking about, a significant effort must be made in the diagnosis phase, when specific structural problems are identified and understood. The benefits of this are reaped tenfold in targeted, impactful and sustainable change. Of course, this means that ready-made culture change management templates are not going to be of much use here, no matter how slick PowerPoint presentations are. They just don't reflect reality.

The effectiveness of these changes to people's lived experience is a substantive area of inquiry, yet this is often not incorporated into change programs.[20] I believe this is due to the fact that when a big culture problem is called out, there is pressure to announce big culture reform. This might appease many, but it may also lead to the absence of tangible change for those living the day-to-day reality of an organisation.

A good example of a change at the individual level was the daily practice that became required of staff at Rio Tinto. The mining group mandated a 'safety share' at the beginning of every meeting, no matter how big or small it was, or what level of the organisation it involved—whether attendees were cleaning staff or executives. This involved someone volunteering a safety risk they might have recently seen, and not necessarily in the company—they might have spotted it on their way to work, or at their child's soccer practice. This decision reinforced safety messages and instilled a safety culture, one strengthened by a process of constant learning and reflection.

As another example, some decades ago, in the wake of a series of catastrophic aircraft crashes that involved a horrendous loss of life, the aviation world ushered in the Crew Resource Management model and a global system of 'no blame' Air Safety Occurrence Reports. This allowed crew members, air traffic controllers, maintenance staff, indeed anyone working in the aviation network, to initiate an Air Safety Occurrence Report that went into a global alert system, and airlines were able to act on these warnings immediately. In addition, the management model ushered in a new set of behaviours, standards and expectations for conduct on the flight deck. Over time, this completely dismantled the longstanding practice of hero-worshiping the pilot, replacing it with respectful deference to the whole crew, combined with the democratisation of knowledge. Some would describe this as a culture change, but it derived from a small change that eventually flattened the power structures in aviation and introduced a new type of aviation professionalism.

~

How will the ADF, or the public, know when Special Force's culture has changed? Will it be when the risk of atrocities being committed is significantly reduced? Perhaps it will be when there is greater reporting of misconduct, although reporting presents a conundrum. When a robust complaints management system is implemented, does an increase in reporting signal improvement? Or if this initiative is part of a broader program of culture reform, should one expect complaints to be minimal?

Unfortunately, there is no easy answer here. However, it helps to accompany a program of reform with a theory of change, which is basically a detailed explanation and illustration of how and why a desired change is supposed to occur in a specific situation. It is especially concerned with figuring out what has been referred to as the 'missing middle' between what a change program or initiative does—its actions or interventions—and how these help achievement of the desired outcomes. It accomplishes this by first identifying the long-term goals and then working backwards from there to decide all of the conditions that must be met, or outcomes, for the goals to be realised.

Addressing misconduct, the problematic distribution of power and faulty accountability mechanisms in Special Forces will require deep structural change and will need to be reinforced by targeted actions. Anything less will only result in temporary change—or no change at all. To be sustainable—that is, to outlast consecutive leaders at all levels—these changes have to challenge power structures and the scaffolding that holds them in place throughout the organisation.

BEYOND CULTURE

Going back to the questions I posed at the start of this book, my experience has taught me that the word 'culture'—its meaning, history and power— really matters, and this needs to be understood lest one fall into the trap of a culture malaise. I've learnt that power should not be framed as a component of culture; rather, it should be examined *instead* of culture. I also understand that accountability goes hand-in-glove with power and needs to be unpacked, called out, made explicit and transparent, and that dismantling the organisational scaffolding that holds dysfunctional power structures in place requires small, sustainable changes rather than what's offered by the so-called flagship culture change programs. And I believe that one needs to have an underpinning theory of change in order to monitor and evaluate progress toward the desired changes.

These realisations are important because the construct of culture within organisational change has become confused and confusing. It is a popular go-to when it comes to reporting stories of misconduct in organisations, and is used as a catch-all term to explain why bad things are happening. But unfortunately it is also used to justify such issues. Culture is sometimes presented as an independent phenomenon that underpins practices at the individual level, the level of day-to-day experience, and bolsters the overarching norms at the organisational level. Simultaneously, it is positioned as something that can be set or shaped, most often by senior leaders. All of which means that rather than assisting in the diagnosis of organisational misconduct, for example, culture can instead muddy our understanding of why and how an issue manifested in the first place. Worryingly, it can also obscure our ability to hold the right people, and the right organisational structures, to account.

Accountability mechanisms take many forms. Researchers have distinguished formal from informal accountability, hierarchical from horizontal, mandatory from voluntary, political from administrative, as well as financial, performance and procedural accountability. As a result, references to accountability are often subjective and fiercely debated. When certain commentators call for more accountability from the top brass in Defence over the war crimes allegations and the associated culture, they are referring to formal, hierarchical accountability. If the assumption is that the senior leader of the organisation ultimately sets the culture, then this makes sense. However, culture acts to blur accountability in this situation. The assumption that senior leaders alone set the prevailing culture is faulty, and if the described culture does not resonate with the majority, then questions of collective accountability become displaced. There are many unaccountable pockets of power and influence in today's complex governance structures, such as where policies are enforced by networks, autonomous entities, public–private partnerships, or regulatory experts. There are accountability paradoxes and deficits.

Culture can be a convenient truth. It conveys everything needed when defining a problem: bad conduct, something entrenched and all-encompassing, a lack of transparency, an absence of accountability and so on. The label also shames the organisation, and it often dictates the fate of the organisation and its leaders. Furthermore, the rhetoric of culture reform—the default solution to a culture problem—sounds promising: cultural transformation, organisational improvement, institutional change. The change management tools and strategies that accompany such initiatives certainly lower the collective heart rate of senior leaders: there are linear change journey maps, neat stakeholder matrices, key performance indicators colourfully cascading down an Excel spreadsheet. Sadly, it's all a façade. The thrill of a slick PowerPoint deck quickly dissipates as the culture change backlash begins.

There is a need to challenge culture as the default organisational problem diagnosis and solution. Instead, an examination of how power operates formally and informally in organisational networks, and the identification of climates that are conducive to misconduct, will not only establish the risks and barriers to change efforts, but importantly they will highlight what needs to be done.

Culture reform efforts are often as much focused on improving organisational performance as they are about rebuilding public or government trust. Many issues are associated with cover-ups, so transparency is key. And a core component of delivering on increased transparency is demonstrating accountability, be it individual or collective. To do this, sufficient time and effort has to be invested in defining exactly what is meant by accountability. The benefits here are twofold: accurate data collection where it is needed most, and a greater ability to communicate improvements in accountability to those whose trust has been breached.

Culture also cannot be changed without changing structures. By structures, I am referring to the *things*, not the *people*, that wield power. These things—laws, policies, remuneration models, career management processes—are far more enduring in their ability to affect people's behaviours and values than any individual leader. You can have a stated organisational value of 'teamwork', but if your promotion and reward processes privilege individual achievements, then this value will be consistently undermined.

Boldly stated transformative change programs may mean big bucks for those assisting in their implementation and project management. They may spawn big promises that appeal to journalists and Senate Estimates committees. But they so often fail to deliver. They fail because they don't take into account how power and influence operate, nor the networks in which they operate, nor the criticality of those who influence rather than those who have the authority of a leadership position. Small, tangible changes are more effective—initiatives that can be tailored to different contexts, climates and relationships; plans that can be implemented in a network rather than in a command structure.

The consequences of acting without having asked the right questions creates more organisational risk. Failures in culture change efforts do not necessarily reflect the authority or willingness for change. It's more that the capacity to change is impeded by structures that hold it back, and by an inability to challenge the distribution of power, knowledge or resources. The ongoing frustration some leaders and organisations feel at change not taking hold, or improvements not being commensurate with the effort, time and money that's been invested in trying to create them, is likely because the same tools are being used time and time and time again. The solution is to ask different questions, and to stop leaning so heavily on culture.

~

The allegations of war crimes committed by Special Forces soldiers will continue to challenge the identity of individuals, communities, and our nation. A sense of change will only be achieved when the central issues are no longer simply designated as 'cultural' but are more specifically defined, and when blame does not ricochet between the various levels of Defence. Culture can help to summarise and signpost problems, but beyond that its effectiveness is limited—indeed, it blurs accountability and action.

Later this year, the new Office of the Special Investigator will address the potential criminal matters raised by the IGADF inquiry and report, this being the reason it was established. It will investigate the allegations, gather evidence, and, as needed, make referrals for prosecution. At the same time, a separate and independent Oversight Panel will, in the words of a prime ministerial press release, 'provide oversight and assurance of Defence's broader response to the Inquiry relating to cultural, organisational and leadership change'.[21] These next steps are critical if we are to ensure that the conduct of individuals, organisations and their leaders is ethical, empathetic and empowering.

ACKNOWLEDGEMENTS

This book is a collection of many ideas and insights gained over a long period of time while doing organisational ethnography. I would like to thank the brilliant team at Rapid Context who have been a collective brains trust, support network, and above all an incredible group of thinkers, writers, researchers and change-makers.

I would also like to acknowledge the leaders I have had the opportunity to work with over the last decade who have entrusted me with some of their most difficult and sensitive issues, and who have been true partners in bringing about change. Thank you for trusting me while I asked endless questions, for not expecting me to be good at creating PowerPoint diagrams, for sitting comfortably with me amongst the ambiguity, and for listening to and acting on what I had to say at the end of it.

Thank you to my partner, Jerome, who has trekked many conceptual mountains and glaciers by my side and never left me wanting.

And to my children, Joseph, Zara and Lily, who will no doubt never use the word 'culture' without having a visceral reaction, thank you for your genuine and loving encouragement.

NOTES

1   Joshua Rothman, 'The Meaning of Culture', *The New Yorker*, 2014, https://www.newyorker.com/books/joshua-rothman/meaning-culture (viewed March 2021).

2   Susan Wright, '"Culture" in Anthropology and Organizational Studies', in *Anthropology of Organizations*, Routledge, London, 1994, p. 4.

3   Australian Government, Department of Defence, *Pathway to Change: Evolving Defence Culture*, 2017, https://www.defence.gov.au/pathwaytochange/ (viewed March 2021).

4   *Inspector-General of the Australian Defence Force Afghanistan Inquiry Report* (public release version), 2020, https://afghanistaninquiry.defence.gov.au/sites/default/files/2020-11/IGADF-Afghanistan-Inquiry-Public-Release-Version.pdf (viewed March 2021).

5   Clausewitz, Carl von, *On War*, ed. and trans. by Michael Howard, Peter Paret and Bernard Brodie, Princeton University Press, Princeton, NJ, 1984.

6   Samantha Crompvoets, *Special Operations Command (SOCOMD) Culture and Interactions: Perceptions, Reputation and Risk*, February 2016, https://afghanistaninquiry.defence.gov.au/sites/default/files/2020-11/SOCOMD-Culture-and-Interactions-Perceptions-Reputation-and-Risk-Feb-16.pdf (viewed March 2021).

7   Ibid.

8   Stjepan Meštrović, *Trials of Abu Ghraib: An Expert Witness Account of Shame and Honor* (1st edn), Routledge, Philadelphia, 2007.

9   Donald Palmer, *Final Report: The Role of Organisational Culture in Child Sexual Abuse in Institutional Contexts*, Royal Commission into Institutional Responses to Child Sexual Abuse, Sydney, 2016, https://apo.org.au/sites/default/files/resource-files/2016-11/apo-nid70928.pdf (viewed March 2021).

10 M Aleksovska, T Schillemans and S Grimmelikhuijsen, 'Lessons from Five Decades of Experimental and Behavioral Research on Accountability: A Systematic Literature Review', *Journal of Behavioral Public Administration*, vol. 2, no. 2, 2019, https://doi.org/10.30636/jbpa.22.66 (viewed March 2021).

11 Stephen Keith McGrath and Stephen Jonathan Whitty, 'Accountability and Responsibility Defined', *International Journal of Managing Projects in Business*, vol. 11, no. 3, 2018, pp. 687–707, https://eprints.usq.edu.au/34150/19/Accountability%20and%20responsibility%20defined%20-%20author%20post-print%20version%20with%202ECs.pdf (viewed March 2021).

12 Stjepan Meštrović, *Trials of Abu Ghraib: An Expert Witness Account of Shame and Honor* (1st edn), Routledge, Philadelphia, 2007.

13 Henrich Greve, Donald Palmer and Jo-Ellen Pozner, 'Organizations Gone Wild: The Causes, Processes, and Consequences of Organizational Misconduct', *The Academy of Management Annals*, vol. 4, no. 1, 2010, pp. 53–107, https://www.researchgate.net/publication/233356005_Organizations_Gone_Wild_The_Causes_Processes_and_Consequences_of_Organizational_Misconduct (viewed March 2021).

14 *Inspector-General of the Australian Defence Force Afghanistan Inquiry Report* (public release version), 2020, https://afghanistaninquiry.defence.gov.au/sites/default/files/2020-11/IGADF-Afghanistan-Inquiry-Public-Release-Version.pdf (viewed March 2021).

15 Ibid., p. 113.

16 Australian Government, Department of Defence, *Review of the Defence Accountability Framework*, January 2011, p. 11, https://www.defence.gov.au/

Publications/Reviews/Black/black_review.pdf (viewed March 2021).

17   Australian Government, Department of Defence, *Pathway to Change: Evolving Defence Culture*, 2017, p. 10, https://www.defence.gov.au/pathwaytochange/ (viewed March 2021).

18   Australian Human Rights Commission, *Review of the Treatment of Women in the Australian Defence Force, 2011–12*, https://humanrights.gov.au/our-work/sex-discrimination/defence-review-home (viewed March 2021).

19   Audre Lorde, 'The Master's Tools Will Never Dismantle the Master's House', in *Sister Outsider: Essays and Speeches*, Crossing Press, Berkeley, CA, 1984, pp. 110–14.

20   Margaret Heffernan, *Beyond Measure: The Big Impact of Small Changes*, Simon and Schuster, New York, 2015.

21   Prime Minister Scott Morrison, 'Statement on IGADF Inquiry', press release, 12 November 2020, https://www.pm.gov.au/media/statement-igadf-inquiry (viewed March 2021).

IN THE NATIONAL INTEREST

Other books on the issues that matter: